LEARNING FROM THE LAND

Yami Lester

Edited by Petronella Vaarzon-Morel
Illustrated by Julie Carter

IAD Press
Alice Springs

First published as *Pages From An Aboriginal Book: History And The Land* in 1982 by the Institute for Aboriginal Development
Reprinted 1984, 1988
Rebound and reprinted 1990
This edition published in 1995; Reprinted 1998
IAD Press
PO Box 2531
Alice Springs
NT 0871
Phone: 08-8951 1311
Fax: 08-8952 2527

Below is straight 10pt (above is slightly larger, to match bromide..)

First published as *Pages From An Aboriginal Book: History And The Land* in 1982 by the Institute for Aboriginal Development
Reprinted 1984, 1988
Rebound and reprinted 1990
This edition published in 1995; Reprinted 1998
IAD Press
PO Box 2531
Alice Springs
NT 0871
Phone: 08-8951 1311
Fax: 08-8952 2527

Contents

Introduction 1
1. Journeys Over The Land 3
2. A Boy's Education 12
3. Yankunytjatjara Memories - Conflict Over Land 26

Introduction

In our culture, we don't have books or tapes or anything written down. We have to talk to people older than us who can tell us stories of the land, about the history of our people, how people lived in this country and about the first contact with non-Aboriginals.

Aboriginal culture cannot be separated from the land. On the land are stories, Aboriginal stories that explain why people, rock holes, the hills and the trees came to be there. The land is full of stories. Every square miles is just like a book, a book with a lot of pages, and it's all a story for the children to learn. The old people always tell stories about it, and at an early age the children start learning from that land.

The land holds the people together. The people lived there together and they enjoy the land and know the stories of the land. They know where the rock holes and waterholes are, and they go hunting on the land. The relationship with the land is part of their life. It's their spiritual meaning. They feel sad and get sick if something happens to their place.

In the wapar the land was made. Our culture, the language, the land we live in, our relationship with people and the religious system that controls our everyday life, comes from the wapar. The land is full of the stories.

In Aboriginal society, stories are told for children to learn the culture. And while the children sometimes listen to their mother or their father talking at night around a campfire, they often travel with their parents over the land.

I am going to tell you, firstly, about my childhood journeys and secondly, about some of the experiences of my people.

Chapter One

Journeys Over The Land

Station Days

When I was a little boy, my mother worked for Phil Giles on Wentinna, a sheep and cattle station in the north of South Australia. She worked at the house and my father, the old bloke Kantji, did the cattle work. There weren't very many Aboriginal people there, just a few working for rations and some sitting down in the camp.

There was no school there and my uncle Bill and myself used to hang around the homestead and mess around with the chooks and the nanny goats. We were just kids, just messing around. Near the house were a couple of date trees. One used to bear fruit, and my mother, or uncle Bill's mother, used to rake the ground up for the fruit to drop in a strong wind on the nice clean ground. Bill and I used to be there first, before it had a chance to drop, and we picked the fruit and took it away to have a good feed. We couldn't work out why they always picked on us; but they saw our tracks on the nice clean dirt.

On another time in Wentinna, water tanks were put at the main camp. One day Bill and I were playing around with stones, and a stone dropped down the tank, worked its way to the tap and blocked the opening, so that when you turned the tap on, the water couldn't come through. Well, Phil Giles had an argument with Bill and me, and gave us a hiding. My father was wild with him, and so they both had a 'box-on'. My father threw his job in, pulled out of the station, and we all went out to the bush, walking.

We had two really good dogs, both very good hunters. One was called Tinker and the other one Rover. We travelled west from Wentinna Station, and when our tea and sugar ran out we lived on kangaroos and water. It was alright for the old people but I was used to having a cup of billy tea you know!

I don't know how long we were out that way, but we lived on soakages, waterholes and water on the clay pans. One day Kantji, the old fella, went out hunting with the two dogs. I was with my mother and she was getting witchetty grubs. It was getting late, the sun was going down and it was getting really dark. The old man wasn't home. We were in the hills with a creek running down into the valley. My mother was really worried and she was sitting up when I was trying to go to sleep, when we heard the footsteps of a horse in the distance. We were scared and thought: 'It might be Mr. Giles coming'. Then the horse gave an neigh, and making loud noises, he kept on coming closer until he came past our camp, on a well-worn track there.

Well, it was just one of the wild horses that had got lost and was looking for its mates, I think. Mother was saying that she thought Tjilpi (old man) might have had some difficulties, he may not have found the way back in the dark, because that was only the second night that we had camped there. But Kantji had followed that wild horse, thinking that the track it was on might go past our camp. I don't know how long it was after the horse had gone past, but it was a fair while after when my father arrived back. He had with him a kangaroo all cooked and cut up, and we were happy again.

After a while we came back to the station, and Kantji got a job again, looking after the cattle and shepherding sheep. They would be trucked from Wentinna to Oodnadatta. Sometimes Kantji used to walk the sheep while we had a ride on the wagons pulled by camels.

From Wentinna we moved down to Mt. Willoughby where Kantji worked for a while, then on south-east to Evelyn Downs. From Evelyn Downs we travelled to Arckaringa where Kantji shepherded sheep and did some shearing. I used to like the shearing times. After the sheep were sheared, the wool was picked up by a machine and placed in big hanging bags. When the bags were full, they got all the kids and threw them in to walk on the wool backwards and forwards until the wool was pressed down. Then they'd get us out again, make the bags nice and tight, put the clips on the bags and send them to Oodnadatta. From Oodnadatta they'd go down on the train to Adelaide.

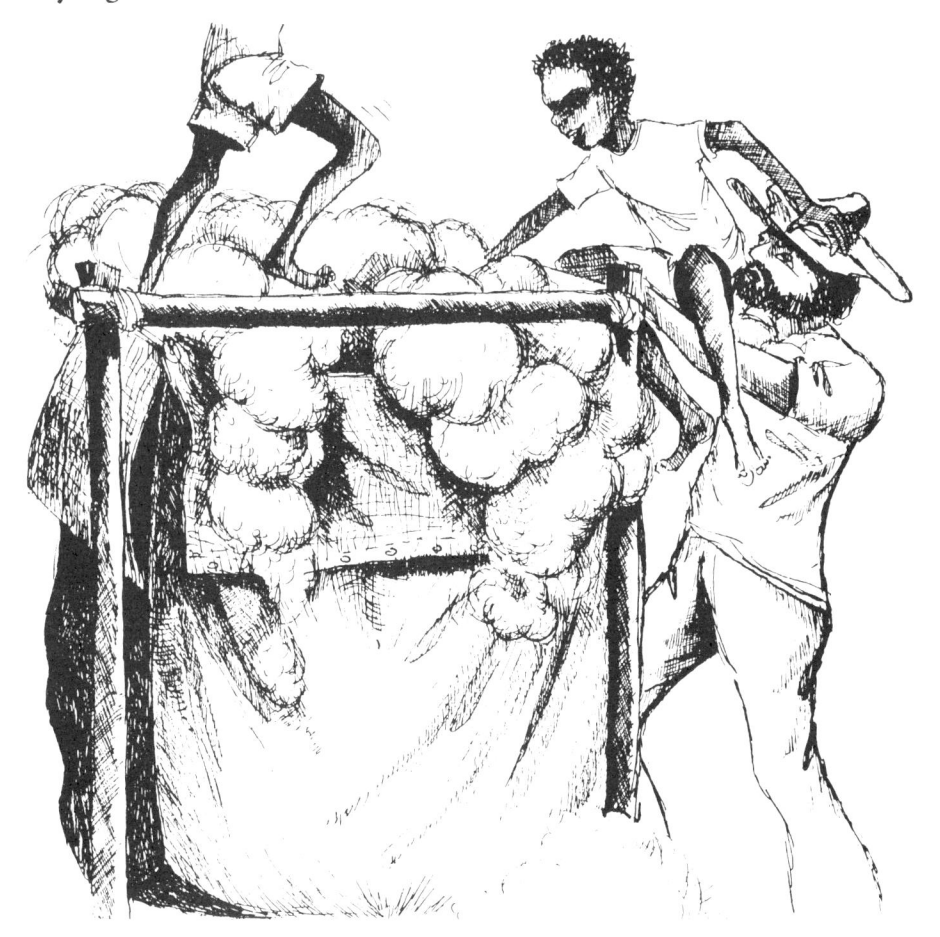

From Arckaringa we'd ride back on the trucks to Wentinna and from there we'd walk to Wallatinna, south of Granite Downs. We'd follow the creek up to the hills and walk across the bush, where our people knew the little places and were able to find water in the rockholes. However, before travelling out over the drier areas they'd wait for the thunder-storms to bring the rain to fill the rockholes, claypans and swamps.

We'd travel with about seven families, mothers, fathers and children.

Chapter 2

A Boy's Education

At a place near Wintja, we came to a swamp with a lot of water lying around. We sat down there for a while and lived on wild animals, grass seeds and different types of bush tucker - kampurampa, wild tomatoes (yellow fruit) and maku, witchetty grubs. At this time our mothers had billy cans of course, because the white fellas were around in our country. To save water for the journey ahead, the women would fill the billy cans with water and then, taking a special grass, they'd form it into the shape of a ring and put it on top of the water, right to the top of the billy can. When you drank you had to take a small sip holding your teeth partly closed so that you didn't take too much. In this way water was saved for us. If you placed the grass on the water like that, it would keep for longer, instead of the sun shining directly onto the water and evaporating it. Water was also carried in big tins and four-gallon drums cut in half. I can remember one lady walking along, balancing a drum full of water on her head.

We travelled onto a place where I was born called Walatjatanya. Here the water lay in soakages in the creek bed itself, so that you had to dig in the sand to get the water out. We spent a couple of days and nights there and then walked to Wallatinna homestead, the lease of which was owned by old Tommy Cullinan. A lot of Yankunytjatjara people were there so we sat down for a time, while Kantji worked as head stockman. It was here as a young fellow that I learnt about hunting. My uncle showed us how to track.

In one game he'd tell us to put our heads down and not look while he walked around softly, and then came to a standstill. We had to try and find his track and the way he went, to where he was standing. He'd say: 'You know where I'm standing; can you pick which way I walked to get here?' We'd try and pick the way, but we'd often miss.

The others would say: 'Oh, he went this way; he put one foot on this rock, then onto the stick and the grass'.

We'd be able to tell by the grass, because if you put your foot on it you sort of squash the grass, and that's how you're supposed to pick it; and my uncle would say in Yankunytjatjara: 'Very good'.

There were many other games he showed us. In another one he got some bark off a tree, cut it into a round shape and threw it on the ground making out that it was a kangaroo. With our little spears we had to try and hit the bark as my uncle threw it along the ground. Some of the kids were pretty good, they'd throw the spear really hard while my uncle sometimes jumped; then you'd throw your spears under the thing or aimed a little bit higher. That was our training for hunting kangaroos. I was maybe eight or nine then, a little kid.

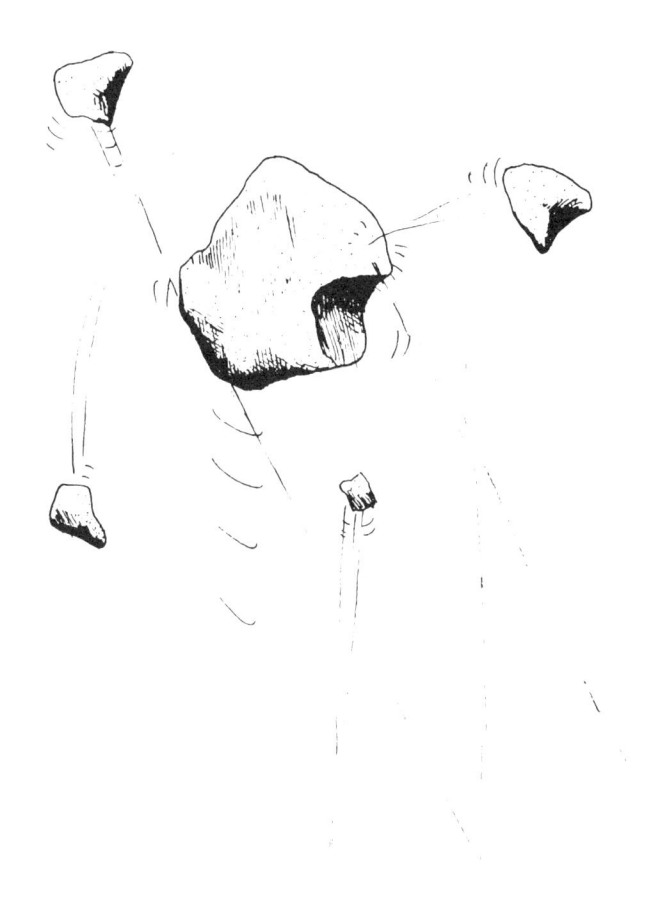

At another time my uncle said; 'I'm going to throw this stick up in the air and you've got to try and hit it. No spears this time, only stones'.

Sometimes he'd throw a bigger rock in the air, heavier than the ones we'd have and we'd have to try and hit it. If you hit it the men would say; 'Oh, good shot; you'll be right. You won't starve'.

Then they'd take us out and say: 'Right, we've got to show you what to do if there was a war, a tribal war, and the fight is on'. The spears we'd use to practise for this were made of plants. You'd flatten the end with a rock to make it soft and blunt. Then my uncle would line up the kids and say: 'Right, you kids, try and get me'. He'd stand there with only a woomera and we'd throw the spears and try and hit him. We'd aim for the rib cage, avoiding the head so as not to hit him in the eye. Moving his body but not his feet, he'd move out of the way or sometimes he'd move his feet a little, all the time watching the spears. He'd have maybe seven kids all throwing spears at him at once, and we just couldn't catch him. Then it would be our turn to stand there and try and dodge the spears from the others. Sometimes we'd miss them, and other times we'd get hit, and uncle would say: 'You're no good. If you ever fight with another tribe, you'll be no good'. Our cousins, brothers and uncles would show us all these things.

When you travelled along with your fathers or mothers they'd be teaching you, telling which type of food you could eat and which was for the animals; the names of the plants like the little berries on the mulga trees. Each plant has a name. They'd show the bad tucker to you and you'd learn not to touch it; it's only for the kangaroos and other animals. The mothers taught the girls in the same way about food; where to look for honey ants and how to dig for them and get the honey ants without busting them, or it might be to do with grass seeds. The women have special names and stories for this food, and the men have stories to do with hunting emus and kangaroos. The kids learn like that. They'll tell stories not only to do with the land, but also stories about how people should behave.

The men would often take us hunting with them. They'd catch a kangaroo and show us how to break the legs and open the stomach in the proper way, then how to tie the kangaroo, making it into a bundle to carry.

We call this 'Nyutini'. You'd tie the two back legs against the tail, then put all of them through the front legs and tie them together, making it just right to sit on your head, to carry it easily. If you make the bundle too big it would push your head down, so it had to be just right. This is the Yankunytjatjara way. Our fathers, grandfathers, cousins and brothers all do it in the same way. You must learn to do things correctly; you can't do them wrong. Other people can see if you aren't doing things in the right way and if you aren't there will be trouble for you or a member of your family as a result. We'd be frightened of that.

We walked from Wallatinna to Mimili where we lived for a while. Near Mimili is Victory Well; we call it Parulpir. It is a water course with many kangaroos living there. The men would say: 'Come on, you young fellas, we've got to show you how to hunt with spears'. There's hunting in a group, then there's hunting in pairs and by yourself, but this time we went in a group.

The women played their part. All the adult women and young girls went in the opposite direction to us with the west wind blowing towards all the men down on the east side. The men hid behind a mulga tree and a wood stand they'd made, and waited. I didn't know what was going on with all the women, we just left them there and they worked it out. They'd gone right up the top end and started frightening the kangaroos by calling out. When a big mob of kangaroos started coming towards us, the women made noises to let us know. I was right at the back of all the men, and this bloke in front of me said: "You watch me". Then the kangaroos came, flat out, going like mad because all those women and girls had frightened them. When a kangaroo came towards this bloke that I was behind, and he was ready to throw a spear, he moved his foot a little off the ground. The kangaroo saw that and jumped up high. While he was up in the air the man threw a spear right into the side of his chest.

When the kangaroo is in mid-air, he can't see anything and when the spear is coming at him, he just can't do anything, but if the kangaroo was hopping along, and you just threw the spear he could see that and would touch the ground, stop and turn. So the men cheat, they just move their foot, then the kangaroo jumps real high and while he is in mid-air they throw the spears and get their tucker. They have to do that so that they can get food, you know.

The men learnt these skills as kids, throwing stones, sticks, spears and using woomeras. Their arms became trained through this exercise and they became pretty accurate in aiming for things. So that's how they caught kangaroos. We had the biggest feed that day; oh, there were kangaroos everywhere!

Hunting in pairs is another hunting method they use. While the kangaroo is having a feed, one person watches from behind a tree and the other falls back and circles around, coming up behind the kangaroo. When the one watching behind the tree is confident that he can get the kangaroo, the other person will move so that the kangaroo will see him, get up, and hop away towards the other man who'll throw the spear at him.

When hunting by yourself, you have to sneak up to the kangaroo. Windy days with a really strong north wind blowing are the best times to hunt by yourself. You stand behind the kangaroo so that your scent isn't carried to him. But the kangaroo is very intelligent and if he thinks that he can hear something different to the wind blowing and the noise of the trees - the sound of a man holding a spear ready - then he will look straight away. He won't look in the direction the wind is coming from, but the other way, because he knows that if it was on the other side that he would have smelt whatever it was. So he looks straight out and he'll see you; then he'll look again to make sure and he'll say to himself: 'Sure enough, it's a bloke with a spear', and he'll hop away. You'll lose him and you won't have a feed that night.

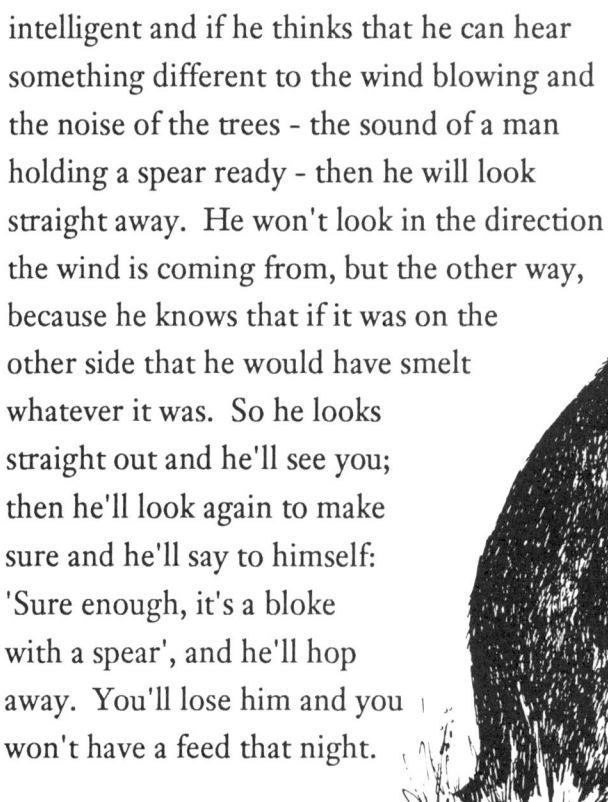

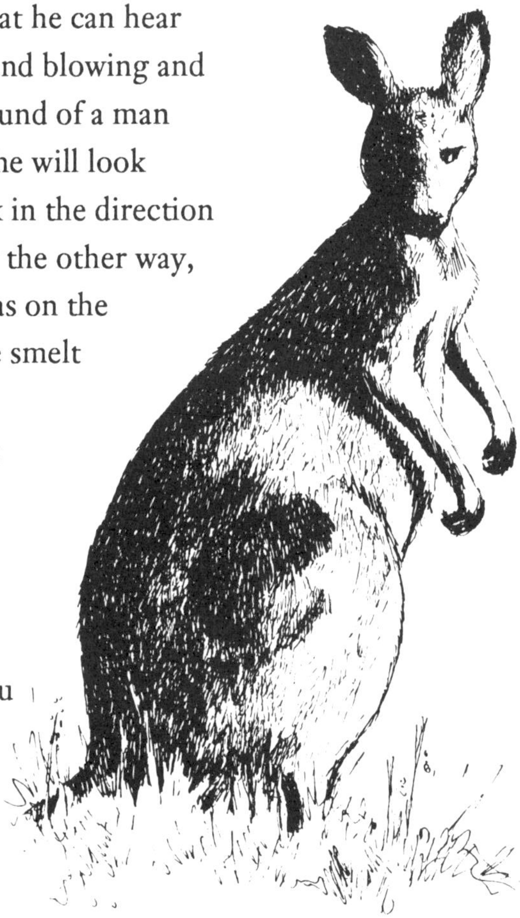

Late in the evening when the sun is going down, the experienced hunter will go against the sun so that it is in the kangaroo's eyes and he can't see. The hunter can get very close to throw the spear then, but if he was away from the sun, the kangaroo could easily see him.

The rock wallabies are easy to get. They live on the hills, hiding in the spinifex or behind some trees. They'll come out on to an open flat rock and look around, if you throw a rock in amongst them in the trees, then you can spear them.

The kangaroo is a bit cunning.

While the men hunted kangaroos, the women looked for other food, like goannas and honey ants. Honey ants come in good seasons, after the rain brings out the blossom, for the honey ants to collect the honey. There is another type of honey on the young mulga tree; it's very nice too. The women and girls gather it from the little branches on the young trees. I can remember in a really good year, not far from Wallatinna at a place called Larry's Well, there was a nice creek with a lot of young mulga trees.

If you looked at it with the sun shining through the branches you could see the honey as liquid running down to the ground, right around the bottom of the tree. There it hardened and so we used to break it up into pieces to eat, or suck on it. We'd break it up, heap it up on the hard ground, cut the leaves off the branches and make a bundle of it for everyone to carry. It was just like carrying meat home. The girls used to carry home a bundle each.

In the old days they used a wooden dish, but when I was there they used an ordinary white fella's dish or a half-gallon drum. First they'd put the water in them and then all the branches with honey on them to soak in the water, and you worked the branches up and down so that the water became sweet with the honey. On the sandhills you find a special grass that you can make soft and rubbery. They used to put it in a wooden dish of sweet water water and everybody would suck the sweetness from it. The women-folk had this food and perhaps goannas or perenti, and the men would come home with kangaroos.

The men shared the meat with the women and the women shared the honey water. Sometimes the men might have nothing after a long walk, because the kangaroos were too quick for them, so the men would eat damper made from the grass seeds, like johnny cakes.

Sometimes there may have been 40 to 50 adults with their families living and moving around in the one area; at other times there was only a wife, husband and kids living on their own or perhaps two brothers and their families. Usually they would spread out over their own countries, one group at Wallatinna, another in Mimili, and other people living further west. When ceremonies were on they all came together in the one place, where there was plenty of food and water. Sometimes there were 80 to 100 people together.

When there was no European school the adults had the children with them all the time and they'd teach them how to talk and how to behave, how to talk to their brothers and uncles, or how to talk to the kids when the kids were growing, then how to talk to teenagers. Until the kids get to a certain age they are treated like little children, but when they became teenagers, uncles talk to them differently, indirectly. We had a word for it 'Tjalpawangkanyi'.

Some of the bedtime stories talk about the proper way to behave. There's a story about how an older brother treats his young brother while he is growing up. He is allowed to talk straight to him; for example, he could ask him to get firewood; 'Can you get some wood?' or 'Get some wood'. However when the younger brother gets to a certain age and that lad is growing and changing, the older brother can only ask him indirectly. 'Oh, I wish I had some firewood; I'd better go and get some'. So the older people will tell you bedtime stories like this, how to be a good 'boyscout' and a good girl.

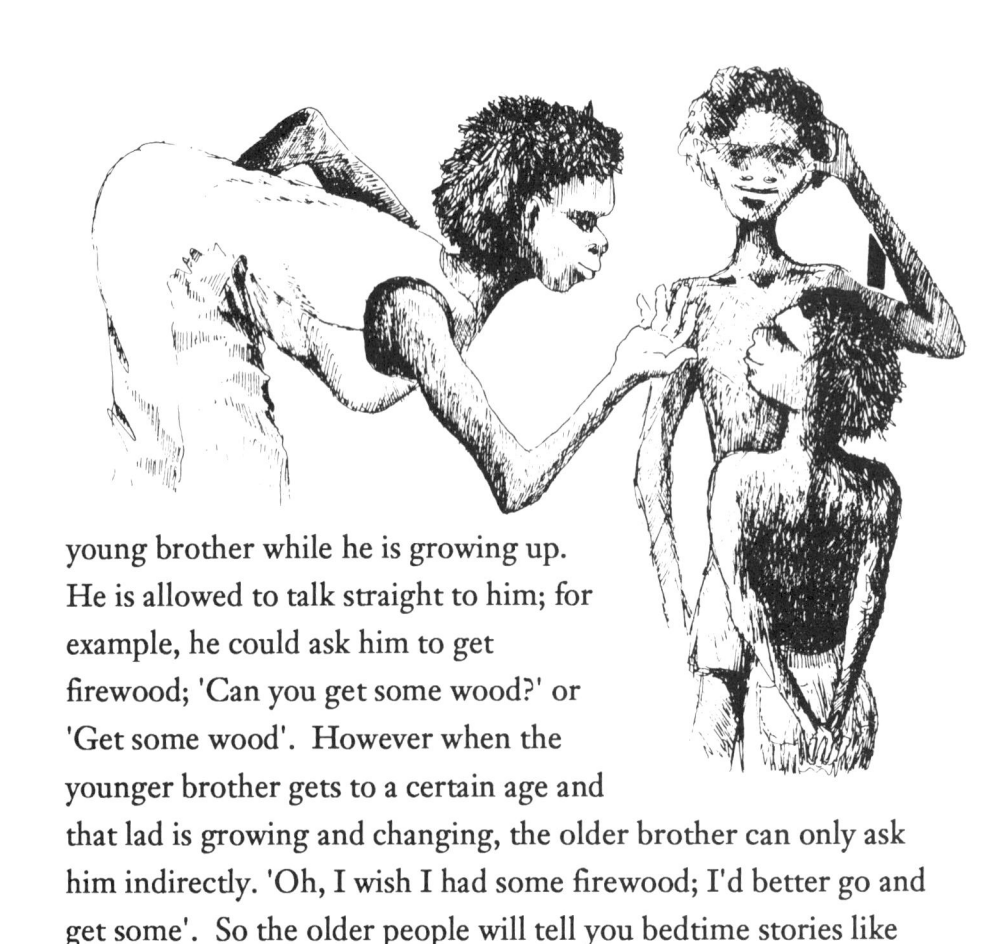

Chapter 3

Yankunytjatjara Memories - Conflict Over Land

As well as teaching us about the land, the grown-ups used to sit down with us and tell us about their experiences when they first came into contact with non-Aboriginals.

When the Yankunytjatjara people first saw sheep, camels and horses they really didn't know what they were and they were frightened.

There were Aboriginal people living all the way to the Western Australian border, when the non-Aboriginals moved in with their cattle and sheep on to the good stretches of land and the waterholes.

The old people remember a fellow called Briscoe who brought sheep up to Betty's Well and left them there.

He used a rifle to help him settle that land, and if the people saw him when they were going for water, they'd be very quick and run away to the hills. He would only allow people to stay there if they worked for him and the other people who came in, walking in their own country, he'd move them on. Betty's Well was sunk by an Aboriginal person who is still living at Indulkana. The people were worried about the cattle drinking up the water supply, as they mainly relied on the rainwater in the springs and soakages.

The people sit down and talk about the things that happened when the whites came into their country; what the white fellow did and what the Aboriginal person did to the white person in return. At one time a Yankunytjatjara man came home after hunting and saw a white bloke having a bath in his water in the rockhole. Worried about his water, the Yankunytjatjara man speared the white man, but he didn't throw the spear to kill him, only to hit him just on some muscles underneath his arm. Well, when he did that the white man ran away; he pulled the spear out of his side and was alright then, but he didn't come back again to find out what was happening.

One story I was told by the old people concerns a policeman who used to come from Oodnadatta, right up to the Everard Ranges and to Mimili Station. The early white men called him up if their sheep were missing, because sometimes the Aboriginals killed their sheep for meat. This policeman had an Aboriginal tracker with him.

Using 'black trackers', policemen often used to round up Aboriginal people, taking them on horseback and camels. Although the police were officially called 'Protectors' of Aboriginal people they were in fact, protecting the Europeans.

The Aboriginal trackers were taken from distant areas, so they wouldn't know the Aboriginal people whom they had to deal with. They knew they were doing wrong, but they'd have to work for the white policeman because otherwise he'd use a gun and chase them on a horse, and try and shoot them down. Some used to run their horse into them and get them in the ankles.

One day the police came up to where a community of Aboriginal people lived. The police, the tracker and the station owner mustered up the Aboriginal people on horseback and herded them to Betty's Well, in Mimili. The tracker asked them: 'Hey, how many sheep do you have?'. The Aboriginal men said: 'No, we didn't have any, it must have been a different group'. They handcuffed the men and chained them together in a long line. They left the women and children at Betty's Well and made the men walk to Victory Well, where the police undid the handcuffs and made the people get wood. After they had finished carting the wood, the policeman counted the men. One had run away and when they couldn't find him the policeman punished another man, giving him a hiding and hitting him with a short chain all over his body. It was a really nasty experience.

From there they were taken all the way to Oodnadatta, which is 200 miles from Mimili homestead. They walked all the way and then were put in jail there. Before they had finished serving their term and were let out, the policeman got a special stockwhip with spiky ends and gave the men a hiding with that whip. They had cuts and bruises and lumps coming up all over them and then they had to walk all the way back to Mimili.

Before the Stuart Highway went through up to the Northern Territory, camels used to come from Oodnadatta and bring a load across. From Oodnadatta they walked to Welbourne Hill, then into Chandler and Granite Downs where there were some white people in the early days. There was no-one living at Mimili, only the Aboriginal people, who used to go to Chandler to trade dingo scalps with the whites, getting tea and sugar in exchange.

There were three brothers who were living there, trying to start off a bit of a sheep station but because of lack of water they had to move around a lot. There were a lot of white people further up north, at the saokages, moving about with sheep, all trying to find a suitable place with water. For a long time others stayed not far from Granite Downs and Kenmore as they had found water there to run the sheep.

Later they started stocking up the cattle station at Mimili and that's when white fellows came and settled down. The Aboriginal people were sitting down there all the time anyway, around the Mimili rockhole and all the little places there on the Everard Ranges where they lived and moved about.

Then from the west there was a drought, and people from the west moved to the east, and they came in contact with Yankunytjatjara people and the white people too. They were Pitjantjatjara people, who came from the west, near the West Australian border and some from the south side of Amata and the Musgrave Ranges.

Aboriginal people in the Yankunytjatjara area started working then for the whites. They started off working by digging wells, cutting timber, mulga and gums and making stockyards. It wasn't until the middle 50's that they cut posts and put in boundary fences. But they used to build holding paddocks earlier and the

Aboriginal people used to put the posts in by hand, all done by axe and shovel. They built the wells with pick and shovel, with two blokes on the windlass and one bloke down the hole whom they'd wind up. And they built roads to the bores.

They took axes and cut the trees down and they burnt the stumps while the white blokes came along in the truck dragging iron and clearing up. They were still doing it when I was a small boy, making roads that way, like that. When they had finished they would get some rations, tea, sugar, flour, shirts, trousers and blankets and make it look really good; there might be some pound notes trying to look sort of big.

But by and large Aboriginal people put the work into the land and built those stations.

'Tjunguringkulalanya helpamilala mantaku kala
ngura nganampa kanyila kawalinkunytja wiyangku.'

'Help us come together for the land, so that we will keep our country and not lose it.'